This book is humbly and honorably presented to:

_____

From:_____

Date:_____

Remarks: _____

_____

With deep honor and respect, this book is
dedicated to the men and women who have
served in the Army, the Navy, the Air Force, the
Marine Corps, and the Coast Guard
of the United States of America.

by
David L. Johnston
Design by Dave A. Humphrey
Printed in the United States of America

ISBN: 978-0-692-69390-2
Published by Nothing But The Truth Publications

A TIME TO KILL
A Time To Heal

To every thing there is a season,
And a time to every purpose under the heaven:
A time to be born, and a time to die....
A time to kill and a time to heal.
—Ecclesiastes 3:1–3

A Time to Kill

How could there be a time to kill? Almost everyone knows that one of the Ten Commandments plainly says, *"Thou shalt not kill"* (Exodus 20:13). However, the text literally says, "Thou shalt not commit murder." This proper understanding is further verified by instructions for capital punishments, such as the killing of a murderer.

In the Bible, capital punishment was mandated for capital crimes and was never considered a "cruel or unusual punishment." It's a law, and a law is a rule of action.

There were times when God (as revealed in the Bible) actually required killing—not the taking of an innocent life, but the taking of the lives of incurable evil perpetrators.

When Is the Time to Kill Justified?
Five Biblical Instances

1. When the capital crime of murder has been committed: *"He that smiteth a man, so that he die, shall be surely put to death"* (Exodus 21:12).

2. When the capital crime of kidnapping has been committed: *"And he that stealeth a man, and selleth him, or if he be found in his hand, he shall surely be put to death"* (Exodus 21:16).

3. When the capital crime of rape has been committed: *"If a man find a betrothed damsel in the field, and the man force her, and lie with her: then the man only that lay with her shall die"* (Deuteronomy 22:25).

Adultery and parental abuse were treated similarly in the Old Testament. This should at least indicate to us the seriousness of both adultery and parental abuse. Adultery is a violent crime. It is marital treason. It leads to divorce, the desertion of spouses, and the abandonment of children by one of the parents. It destroys marriages, which destroys families, which destroys the entire foundation of a culture.

4. A time to kill is only authorized when capital punishments are carried out by the proper authorities after lawful due process has occurred: no vigilantism; no taking the law into one's own hands.

The Law Is King

The phrase Lex Rex means the "law is king." Some nations operate in the opposite manner: Rex Lex meaning the "king is law." This choice of fundamental legal philosophy usually separates the civil cultures from the uncivil ones. By "law," we refer to "nature's law," or "God's law." In the United States' Declaration of Independence, proper reference is made to "…the laws of nature and of nature's God." God's law, as represented by the Judeo-Christian faiths, is the source of all moral values.

Separated from law and justice, man becomes monstrous. Law can never be formed out of the tyrant's will. Only the sacred laws of God are capable of demanding proper respect, and respect is what leads to zealous abeyance, with each of us being accountable for our own actions.

Is it just to kill incurable evil perpetrators?

A TIME TO KILL
A Time To Heal

5. It is a completely appropriate time to kill when a "just war" must be fought: Saint Augustine of Hippo argued from Romans 13:4 that God has given "the sword" to government. He coined the term "just war" in his book *The City of God*.

Thomas Aquinas, thirteenth-century philosopher and theologian, gave further definition to the "just war" as follows:
a) The war must be waged by a properly instituted authority.
b) The war must be for good and just purposes, not for self-gain. These good and just purposes included the recovery of lost territory or lost goods or the punishment for an evil deed perpetrated by a government, army, or civilian populace.
c) The restoration of peace must be the primary motive.

And thus, civil nations attempt to execute war—a very uncivil undertaking—in a civil manner, based on: 1) just cause; 2) just conduct during the war; and 3) a just conclusion to the war.

Over the centuries and decades, more details of what constitutes a just war, or a just killing—such as killing in self-defense, preventive war actions against aggressors, and punishment of the guilty—have been added. Proper rules of engagement have been formed by numerous conventions to protect civilian life, and certain mass forms of genocide are expressly forbidden. Eventually, a criteria of just war theory has been generally accepted. Three categories have emerged: *Jus ad bellum*, or the right to go to war; *Jus in bello*, or the right and proper conduct within a war; and *Jus post bellum*, or justice after the war. As you can well imagine, volumes of books, perhaps even an entire library, could be written on this subject. However, there are a few things that should be noted about modern warfare that directly relate to the principles of a just war.

The Geneva Conventions consisted of four conventions, and three protocols requiring international agreements that determined the treatment of civilians and prisoners of war (POWs), protection for the wounded, protocols for humanitarianism, and the treatment of non-combatants. These conventions applied to "declared wars" but we continue to honor them even when dealing with non-governmental organizations (NGOs).

The Hague Conventions, on the other hand, dealt with the methods of warfare, banning projectiles that spread asphyxiating gasses, including the discharge of projectiles and explosives from balloons.

Currently, however, it seems that there are no rules. We're currently involved in what is referred to as "Fourth-Generation Warfare." In this generation, anything goes: the killing of innocents; the sexual assault of captives; the kidnapping of children; the targeting of certain religious groups to behead, burn, or emaciate them, simply because of their chosen form of worship—or for no reason at all except the perpetuation of terror. These incurable perpetrators of evil must themselves be killed, according to the Bible!

Many religious extremists believe in and carry out a "theology of rape,"[1] contending in a twisted way, that Mohammed and the Quran condone the right to rape women and children of conquered territories who are not followers of Islam. Indeed, they actually believe that the raping of unbelievers draws them closer to "god," an act of *ibadah*,[2] or worship attributed to the Quran. This "right to rape" is also used as a recruitment tool, attracting men to join the ranks of their jihadist armies. These sexual conquests become motivating factors in territorial conquests. Terrorists hold sex slaves in warehouses, where "buyers" can view and inspect the women and children being marketed as *sabaya* (slaves).[3] Again, these incurable perpetrators of evil must themselves be terminated!

A TIME TO KILL
A Time To Heal

join their ranks. Suicide missions are common—and even desirable—based on the untrue promises of a false "god" who rewards self-murder in his name.

Our counterterrorism and adaptive counterinsurgency (COIN) strategies are not working—and they will not work. No military force has been able to contain the threat of religious extremism. Their brutal interpretation of sharia—their religious laws— embolden them to conduct unrighteous missions of a horrific nature. They cluster in urban areas and integrate themselves into civilian populations, using women and children as human shields. Our Western ethical values and concerns over collateral damage to civilians puts them virtually out of reach in these conditions. A drone strike here and there may kill a few leaders, but what's needed is their utter annihilation. And our question here is about the ethical dilemma of killing them. Look at the facts and then consider this: Does dealing with terrorism call for a legitimate killing mission?

A TIME TO KILL
A Time To Heal

"They cluster in urban areas and integrate themselves into civilian populations, using women and children as human shields."

If a group of five commit a murder, all five persons deserve the death penalty. If there is an entire invading army, hell-bent on raping, robbing, plundering, killing, and kidnapping innocent people, they all must die. The lives of these incurable perpetrators of evil must be terminated. They must be killed. And not only must they be killed as an act of self-defense, the killing of incurable perpetrators of evil is actually a loving act! It is motivated by love, because it protects and defends the innocents, and it proves love for the perpetrators, because it prevents them from incurring even greater condemnation in the hereafter, for *"it is appointed unto men once to die, but after this the judgment"* (Hebrews 9:27).

he will have to deal with
the consequences of that
hatred later In his own
heart, mind, and soul.

Regardless of the justifications we have cited here for killing, in spite of it being the truly "right thing to do," those who must do the actual killing (in this case, our brave soldiers) are damaged in the process... psychologically, emotionally, socially, and spiritually. Killing is not "natural," and it never feels right. As a result, soldiers often internalize a "just killing" as a "wrongdoing," and therefore they suffer false guilt.

Many of our soldiers return home already maimed and dismembered, without arms or legs; some without their hearing; some without their eyesight; and some even without properly functioning internal organs. Then there are those with traumatic brain injury (TBI). Some never return home because they gave the ultimate sacrifice: their lives. Of those who do return home, most are mentally and emotionally tortured and marred, broken and blemished, traumatized, stressed, and confused.

FREEDOM IS NOT FREE

The killing fields, justified or not, always take their toll. This is why the Bible declares that after the killing, there must be a healing.

A TIME TO KILL
A Time To Heal

Before going further let's be sure we applaud each soldier for his or her service. Go out of your way to thank those who have committed to terminate evil in the world and preserve freedom in America.

Expressing gratitude is a matter of Biblical priciple.

"Render tribute to whom tribute is due, and honor to whom honor is due".
(Romans 13:7)

A TIME TO KILL
A Time To Heal

A Time To Heal

War is hell. A veteran is not simply a person who has served in the Armed Forces, or an older soldier who has seen long years of service. A veteran is a person who has been to hell and back. And many of them have been to hell and back, and back to hell again and again.

Some of us do not have the slightest notion of the real and tangible consequences of such a visit to this kind of hell, especially a long-term visit—months of days spent in the "killing fields." Some of our brave soldiers never return. Politicians are forever parroting accolades about them, but they actually do little or nothing to help our veterans in meaningful ways.

A TIME TO KILL
A Time To Heal

Government departments have turned into cold bureaucracies, plagued with corruption and fraud. The once well-intended system has been bastardized. And the returning soldier suffers endless repercussions from the killings he has committed.

But there is hope for our righteous soldiers! Now comes the insight from the Bible: *"A time to kill, and a time to heal"* (Ecclesiastes 3:3). What an accurate and deep understanding this conveys! Everyone who has had to kill, either rightly or wrongly, must take the time necessary to heal.

A TIME TO KILL
A Time To Heal

According to a report generated by the Department of Veterans Affairs, an average of twenty-two veterans a day commit suicide.[4]

Post-traumatic stress disorder (PTSD) is every veteran's issue. PTSD is a mental, emotional, spiritual, and socially disrupting condition, precipitated by witnessing, experiencing, and/or participating in the horrors of killing. Its symptoms vary from flashbacks to nightmares; from anxiety attacks to uncontrollable thoughts.

A TIME TO KILL
A Time To Heal

Contrary to popular belief, time does not heal all wounds. Veterans of the Vietnam War still hurt today. Unless they are healed, every veteran will carry the damage, the destruction, and the devastation of war to his or her grave.

While PTSD can have other causes, I am limiting my remarks here to the single cause of combat exposure. According to the Mayo Clinic,[5] symptoms may include emotional reactions, such as irritability, angry outbursts, or aggressive behaviors; always being on guard for danger; overwhelming feelings of guilt and shame; self-destructive behaviors, such as drinking and/or fast driving; trouble concentrating; trouble sleeping; and becoming easily startled or frightened...

A TIME TO KILL
A Time To Heal

Experiencing negative feelings about one's self or others; feelings of emotional numbness; a lack of interest in what was once enjoyed; feelings of hopelessness about the future; memory problems; difficulty in maintaining close relationships—and the list goes on and on. All of these can be the result of the *trauma of war.*

Think of the consequences of war that affect marriages and families in America when soldiers return home from the battlefield. Every relationship becomes affected and infected. Severe depression replaces the "entertainment killing," usually featured in video games. But killing was never meant to be entertainment. *Real-life* killing produces *real-life* guilt that must be dealt with.

The elimination of guilt associated with real-life, even justified killing in a time of war, along with the side effects of that guilt, is the major foundation for the soldier's healing. How, then, can this ever take place? Psychologists have offered some "mechanical methods." Here are a few:

Rationalization is an attempt to excuse emotionally intolerable behaviors by explaining them in a seemingly rational manner. Therefore, the true explanation is avoided in order to make the behavior tolerable, or even admirable. However, the conclusion is not persuasive, and it usually leaves the soldier feeling worse than he or she did before.

A TIME TO KILL
A Time To Heal

Regression is a defense mechanism used in "psychoanalytic theory," touted by Sigmund Freud as a reversion back to a former stage of development, rather than handling an issue straightforwardly in a more "adult way." This results in "fixations" and "neuroses." It involves a flight from reality, a blocking of awareness— hardly a "cure," or a "healing."

Sublimation is the transferring of negative impulses into more socially acceptable actions, or into less harmful behaviors. Thus, the new behavior essentially serves as a distraction. For example, "I'm angry, so I will now go out and chop wood." Thereby, aggressions are allegedly diverted into constructive endeavors.

Reaction formation is the development of polar-opposite tendencies. It is a movement from unacceptable, anxiety-producing emotions to calmer, more acceptable behaviors. For example, a person may react to uncleanliness by developing extreme compulsive and exaggerated forms of cleanliness. The problem, however, is that the underlying feelings about uncleanliness still exist.

Disassociation is the attempt to detach, or disassociate, oneself from a known reality. The problem here is that such dissociative phenomena is usually a complete detachment from reality, which relies on creating an imagined, but false reality. Now that person suffers from psychosis and has lost contact with reality, which can lead to bipolar disorders—or even schizophrenia.

A TIME TO KILL
A Time To Heal

Antipsychotic drugs are offered *en masse* as a supposed "fix." However, drugs usually only mask the symptoms and provide no cure at all. The medicalization of mental and social disorders has now become the norm. When will we learn that there is no *chemical cure for a psychological problem?* When will we learn that there is no *psychological cure for a spiritual problem?*

Each of these described strategies are coping mechanisms, not cures. The real issue for the soldier returning from the killing fields is his or her underlying and internalized guilt, whether real or imagined.

A TIME TO KILL
A Time To Heal

There is Someone who is an expert in dealing with guilt—whether real or imagined. He's been doing it for eons of time. It's God. God deals with people, and all of us have guilt. Jesus Christ came to the world to resolve our situations. He is the only effective and efficient means of dealing with guilt.

The apostle Paul, (a former murderer of Christians) was so transformed by Jesus Christ that he become the author of fourteen books of the New Testament. Imagine that!

He wrote this: *"This is a faithful saying, and worthy of all acceptation, that Christ Jesus came into the world to save sinners; of whom I am chief"* (1 Timothy 1:15). If Paul, the "chief of sinners," and a killer, was completely healed, then you can be, too. There are no limits to your future!

So, take heart, soldier! If a former serial killer and religious extremist wrote half of the New Testament in the Bible, think of what God could do through you and how He can affect your future.

Notice that the Scripture we quoted, written by this once-upon-a-time killer, said that this truth is "worthy of all acceptation"—that is, acceptance by *everyone at all times*…and that means by you too, soldier. You need to accept this fact.

The elimination of your guilt, whether real or imagined— *all of it*—can begin right here, right now. For centuries now, the lives of guilt-laden men and women have been transformed…and God can do a complete work of transformation in you as well.

disposal to eradicate and obliterate your guilt—all of it, *forever!* We're talking about God, the Creator of the stars, the heavens, the earth, and everything that dwells upon the earth.

The same God who created something out of nothing can also make nothing out of something. Never doubt that! That is exactly what He will do with your guilt. All of the psychologists or counselors in this world can never compare or compete with Him.

Your solution starts here. It starts now. Accepting this truth will save you years of pain and torment, and years of unnecessary searching.

Often, we try to resolve our own guilt, in other words, we make self-atonement. The historic jungle tribesmen carried short whips tipped with stones, used to beat their own backs! Some added honey to the open lacerations, to encourage insects to bite the opened, bleeding flesh at their leisure. Strange, isn't it? Because as modern men, we're still doing the same thing—just in more sophisticated ways. Self-atonement for guilt is now often demonstrated through self-destructive behaviors, from harming oneself physically to drug abuse, alcoholism, and various other addictions.

Post-traumatic stress disorder (PTSD) is categorized as a mental health disorder, triggered by seeing or experiencing a terrifying event. Over three million new cases are reported in America each year. However, our focus here is not the *medical management* of such a disorder, but its elimination! Behind this "mental disorder" are very negative effects on the spirit and the soul of a person—a human being whom God loves.

There are three main symptoms of PTSD:

1) reliving certain specific events that include memories, flashbacks, and nightmares, with physical manifestations of rapid breathing, heart palpitations, sweating, nausea, and muscle tension;

2) avoiding reminders that could precipitate detachment from others, loneliness, emotional numbness, fear of the future, and loss of interest in life;

3) extreme anxiety, which manifests in sleeping disorders, lack of concentration, jumpiness, over-care, substance abuse, mistrust, self-blame, depression, disconnection, and even suicidal thoughts. Sometimes this is referred to as social intensity syndrome.

We must understand what happens to veterans who return home wounded physically and/or mentally. We must also understand what has happened to them in the war zones. Here's a short list of what they face on a day-to-day basis on a tour overseas:

- Long-term exposure to hatred

- Being under constant threat

- Months of psychological beatings

- Killing of other human beings

- Loss of their true identity

- Long-term estrangement from spouse and other family members

- Harshness in relationships

- Insensitive environment

- Devastation over loss of comrades

- Fear, confusion, and anger

- Interference of political correctness from politicians or American citizens

A TIME TO KILL
A Time To Heal

Unresolved guilt exacerbates the damage.

Internalized guilt can be divided into two categories, and each requires its own separate solution.

A TIME TO KILL
A Time To Heal

Pseudo-guilt is a "fake" and false form of guilt that is still very "heartfelt" and real, but it has no legitimate basis. Pseudo-guilt includes an inner feeling of personal disapproval, even though none of God's moral laws have been broken. Our human intellect cannot be the Supreme Court, but if followed it is very capable of condemnation— and it very often does condemn the innocent.

Pseudo-guilt can be just as damaging as real guilt. We must learn how to deal with both types of guilt: pseudo and real. With pseudo-guilt, the answer is to stand your ground, based on the truth.[6] Soldiers can lose track of their true sense of justice when they are caught up in a just war and fall under the tyranny of false accusations. In this situation, the soldier, or "justified killer," must revert back to the justice that has been assured. This is not accomplished by the mere thought of the justice, but the justice of the killing must be hammered into the heart, soul, and mind of the misled soldier.

A TIME TO KILL
A Time To Heal

One of the words for wisdom used in the book of Proverbs means to "pound in." This fact must be understood. It is no different from the way you had to learn the multiplication table as a child. You walked the floor of your house, saying, "2x2=4, 2x3=6, 2x4=8," etc., until it was finally pounded in! Now you know the answers automatically. Why? Because you pounded them in!

The soldier must take a stand—a long-term stand—by pounding the truth into himself concerning the justice of the killing. Pseudo-guilt will disappear if you continue to stand your ground!

But what if a soldier's conscience still bothers him? The answer is: You *must* learn the difference between offending one's own conscience and breaking the moral laws of God. Your conscience is only as "infallible" as the information fed to it is "infallible." A conscience can be conditioned to insensitivity so that it doesn't bother a person when it should. Conversely, it can also be trained to be *hypersensitive* in an aberrant way, and it bothers a person much, much more than it should.

A TIME TO KILL
A Time To Heal

Your conscience can be conditioned properly or improperly. The proper conditioning of your conscience has occurred when your conscience is in perfect harmony with the moral laws of God—and only those laws: *"The work of the law written in their hearts, their conscience also bearing witness, and their thoughts the mean while accusing or else excusing one another"* (Romans 2:15).

When our conscience coincides with the laws of God, only then will it be able to accurately accuse us or excuse us. Otherwise, our conscience will not be a precise self-adjudicating mechanism—it does not have the tools it needs to do the job. The proper affirmation of your conscience is one of the keys to happiness: *"Happy is he that condemneth not himself in that thing which he alloweth"* (Romans 14:22).

A TIME TO KILL
A Time To Heal

Your conscience, then, must be tuned, adjusted, and maintained so that it is in proper working order. The adjustment of your conscience will lead to the dismissal of *pseudo-guilt* forever.

Now the soldier/killer must still deal with any *real guilt*. Only God Himself is authorized and capable of taking away real guilt. If the war the soldier waged was not a just war, he will have real, heartfelt guilt. Or if a killing he carried out was not a just killing, then the person *will* have real guilt—and for good reason: It was a *real crime*.

If the soldier perpetrated killings that were contrary to the stated justified, ethical rules of engagement, he will have real guilt. If a soldier plunders any scene, taking money, gold, currency, or anything else that would gain him any personal profit from the war, he *will* have real guilt. Real guilt comes from violating the moral laws of God and/or violating a properly tuned conscience. It is real, earned, lasting, haunting, grievous, weighty, intrusive, upsetting, poignant, and painful.

It cannot be forgotten or ignored, dismissed or diminished, erased or eradicated by anyone or anything. It requires an atonement, an atonement of blood, or otherwise it will last for a lifetime.

A TIME TO KILL
A Time To Heal

No drug, no chemical, no rationalization, no reaction formation, no sublimation, no disassociation, *no nothing* can remove the stains from the heart and the spirit of a man...nothing but blood, *the blood of Jesus!*

"Almost all things are...purged with blood (the symbol of death) *and without shedding of blood is no remission"* (Hebrews 9:22). No remission means no forgiveness, no lessening of the pain, no recovery, no cancellation of the debt, no discharge of the penalty, no suspension of the agony, no revocation of the guilt, no pardon, no absolution, no exculpation, no setting aside the blame—just *forever guilt.*

And soldier, you don't want that! You want forgiveness, and not just forgiveness, but cleansing. You need all of it cleansed out of existence. And only Jesus' blood can do that. He's the Best Friend you could ever have. From out of the pages of the Bible, He comes through the centuries to be at your side right now. He comes to forgive and to cleanse and to heal...you!

ATTENTION SOLDIER

To receive mercy, you must give mercy: *"Blessed are the merciful: for they shall obtain mercy"* (Matthew 5:7).

To receive forgiveness, you must give forgiveness: *"For if ye forgive men their trespasses, your heavenly Father will also forgive you: But if ye forgive not men their trespasses, neither will your Father forgive your trespasses"* (Matthew 6:14–15). How wicked, that we would try to collect from God that which we are not willing to give to others.

Without forgiving all your offenders—all of them, all of them, *all of them*—you will live in bitterness, and with bitterness comes continued, nonstop anger, resentment, hatred, vengeance, confusion, and the destruction of your mental health. Bitterness will tear everything apart: your marriage, your children, your friendships, and you.

Forgiveness takes big-ness. Be big, soldier. Forgiveness is voluntarily refusing to collect from others for the damages they have inflicted on you. Forgiveness is not excusing their behavior. It's paying the debt someone else owes. It is not negotiating. It is giving to someone what they have not earned.

And soldier, forgive yourself, or you could spend the rest of your life punishing yourself with self-destructive behaviors. Forgiveness must always come before forgetting. Unforgiveness (bitterness) keeps wounds open for a lifetime. Damage lives on. You will live in self-condemnation and become your own enemy. You'll be on your way to a split-personality or a multiple personality disorder (MPD), renamed by the American Psychiatric Association as DID, dissociative identity disorder. You risk becoming your own enemy. You, your own enemy, will walk with you everywhere you go and accuse you constantly. A very wise but unknown author wrote, "Forgiveness is unlocking the door to set someone free and then realizing you were the prisoner." *Forgive.* Forgiving everyone includes forgiving yourself.[7]

A TIME TO KILL
A Time To Heal

Here's exactly what you should do right now:

1) Bow your head and your heart before God;

2) Talk to Him;

3) Confess (admit) all of your sins and your real guilt;

4) First forgive all of your offenders and then ask for His forgiveness, because every forgiving person who asks, receives (Matthew 7:8);

5) Ask for His cleansing: *"If we confess our sins, he is faithful and just to forgive us our sins, and to cleanse us from all unrighteousness"* (1 John 1:9);

6) Linger with Him as the Holy Spirit applies the blood of Jesus to your heart, your mind, your emotions, your spirit, your whole being, washing you clean, spotlessly clean, all soiling and blemishes taken away.

A genuine confession only needs to be done once. If you indeed repented and authentically asked for forgiveness, you have received it. It's a done deal. That's why you don't need to ask Him for forgiveness again for the same sin (unless you commit the sin again). If, after receiving forgiveness, you still "feel" guilty, that guilt is pseudo-fake guilt and it will never go away by confessing it over and over again. You get rid of fake guilt by standing your ground on the truth that you have indeed been forgiven, cleansed, and restored.

One more thing, soldier: Start walking right! You're under a new command now. "Living by commandment"[8] means that before you decide, speak, or act in any situation, you first check to see whether or not God has a command that applies. If so, you obey that command immediately, joyfully, and without compromise. This is the secret to living right.

Forward March

A TIME TO KILL
A Time To Heal

What about going forward? What about the future...
your future? What if you have flashbacks, and what if
you start to mentally rehearse the terrors, the torments,
and the traumas of the war, the killing fields? The answer
is to hold your ground—to occupy the territory, so to
speak. To occupy is a military term. It means to "take
possession and control of a territory." In your situation, it
is mental ground and emotional territory that you must
control, and it is an already conquered jurisdiction.
Now the task is to keep possession and control the
position. This will take real soldiership.[5]

An interesting insight from the Bible says, *"Endure hardness as a good soldier of Jesus Christ. No man that warreth entangleth himself with the affairs of this life"* (2 Timothy 2:3–4). In other words, take a tough approach and don't go back to your former mental entanglements. Here's how!

1. Recognize the reality of the past. Don't live in denial. Bad stuff did happen, and yes, you may have been in on it.

2. But now replace those thoughts with renewed thoughts, the memory of your forgiveness and cleansing, and the reestablishment of your life. This is not mere "thought replacement." It is *thought completion.*

Soldier, what you did in the past is only part of the story. The rest of the story is that you have now been forgiven, cleansed, and restored to a right mind, a new and right way of thinking. Your new, right way of thinking will automatically produce a new way of feeling. Attitudes will change.[9]

A TIME TO KILL
A Time To Heal

life, for such a healing and recovery.
And soldier, if you've followed the
instructions, you've got it! Jesus Christ
has taken care of your past.

A TIME TO KILL
A Time To Heal

"Old things are passed away;
behold, all things are become new."
(2 Corinthians 5:17)

A TIME TO KILL
A Time To Heal

4. Get a Bible and read it:

"Read it to be wise. Believe it to be safe. Practice it to be holy. It contains light to guide you, food to support you, and comfort to cheer you. It's the traveller's map, the pilgrim's staff, the pilot's compass, the soldier's sword and the Christian's charter. It should fill your memory, rule your heart, and guide your feet. Read it slowly, frequently, prayerfully, meditatively, searchingly, and devotionally. Study it constantly, perseveringly, and industriously. Read it through and through, until it becomes a part of your being and generates faith that will move mountains. It is a mine of wealth, the source of health, and a world of pleasure. It is a mirror to reflect, a hammer to convict, a fire to refine, seed to multiply, a lamp to guide, and food to nourish. It is bread for the hungry, meat for men, and like honey in the desert. It is rain to refresh, a sword to cut, a bow to revenge, gold to enrich, and power to create life and faith."[12]

5. Pray! Prayer is conversing with God. You don't need to dress up your prayers or cloak them with Shakespearean language. You can skip the *thees, thous,* and the *wherefores.* Just talk to God…about everything. You have direct access, through Jesus Christ. Talk to Him. Do it boldly, but respectfully, and reverently. Tell Him what's on your mind. Prayer is a conversation with God. Don't do all the talking—listen, too! At least half of your prayer time should be spent listening, which is the most important part of any conversation. Prayer was meant to be a dialogue, not a monologue.

Prayer is not telling God what to do, but letting Him tell us what to do. Remember, you can't twist God's arm to get Him to do your will. He's now our commanding officer. We do *His* will.

God doesn't mind you checking out what you hear to be sure that He is the One who's speaking to you. In fact, He insists on it. How can we know it is God speaking? a) He will never contradict what He has already declared in the Bible. He will never tell you to lie, cheat, steal, or commit adultery. He has already made that clear in print. b) He will always speak in a manner that reflects His character. He doesn't yell, scream, or throw fits. That's not in His nature.

He speaks lovingly, tenderly, and gently, yet forcefully. No drama, no earthquake, no explosions or firebombs, no drumrolls or loudspeaker system…just a still, small voice: *"The LORD was not in the wind: and after the wind an earthquake; but the LORD was not in the earthquake: And after the earthquake a fire; but the LORD was not in the fire: and after the fire a still small voice"* (1 Kings 19:11–12).

Check out all voices. Jesus put it this way: *"My sheep hear my voice, and I know them, and they follow me"* (John 10:27). If you are a sheep and a follower, you will hear Him. And when you hear Him and confirm by the Bible what you hear, then you must follow and obey Him. Disobedience will make the voice of God grow faint.

6. Get connected to wise comrades, for *"he that walketh with wise men shall be wise."* Do not connect with fools, for *"a companion of fools shall be destroyed"* (Proverbs 13:20).[13] No consorting with the enemy, because associations are contagious: *"Make no friendship with an angry man...lest thou learn his ways"* (Proverbs 22:24–25).

Lock arms with those who are going God's way. We are in a war. Good and evil come face-to-face on the battlefields of our hearts, minds, and friendships. It's God versus Satan, good versus evil, and right versus wrong. Side with those who side with God—no compromise. Allegiance, loyalty, vigilance, and commitment: These are the watchwords. No matter what has happened in the past, it's a new day. Find a church and a group of people who are true!

A TIME TO KILL
A Time To Heal

7. Join the rescue operation: *"How are the mighty fallen, and the weapons of war perished!"* (2 Samuel 1:27). Many mighty men have fallen, some right before your eyes on the battlefield, to the bullet, to the IED, to the grenade, to the booby trap, and the list goes on. Each and every one of them has taken down mighty men. They're gone now. We must mourn our loss and honor their memory. We should most certainly take up the cause of their widows and care for their fatherless children. They were, indeed, the mighty who have fallen, and their weapons of war have perished.

But there are more mighty men who have fallen. They are the living, not the dead. They are not just the wounded in body, the dismembered, and the physically brain-damaged by concussion. They are the veterans who had to kill, but who haven't healed.

They are the men and women you know who have returned from the battlefields and suffer just as you have suffered, but they don't know what you have learned. They are still lost, empty, disillusioned, frightened, lonely, disenfranchised, misunderstood, and without relief from the pains of war. Alcohol and drugs can only mask some of the symptoms. There is no chemical solution for moral and spiritual damage. They need you, soldier. You must become a warrior to the rescue. Leading others down the path you have discovered is now your mission.

Here is how you can do it:

1. Set a Godly example.

2. Tell your story of redemption.

3. Present the truths you've learned.

4. Persuade them to follow Christ, their new officer in command.

5. Bring them into your fellowship of comrades.

6. Encourage them to rescue other soldiers.

Follow these important steps and you will have achieved the vital mission of helping to heal those who have had to kill.

The Fight to the Finish

"God is strong, and he wants you strong. So take everything the Master has set out for you, well-made weapons of the best materials. And put them to use so you will be able to stand up to everything the Devil throws your way. This is no afternoon athletic contest that we'll walk away from and forget about in a couple of hours. This is for keeps, a life-or-death fight to the finish against the Devil and all his angels."

"Be prepared. You're up against far more than you can handle on your own. Take all the help you can get, every weapon God has issued, so that when it's all over but the shouting you'll still be on your feet. Truth, righteousness, peace, faith, and salvation are more than words. Learn how to apply them. You'll need them throughout your life. God's Word is an indispensable weapon. In the same way, prayer is essential in this ongoing warfare. Pray hard and long. Pray for your brothers and sisters. Keep your eyes open. Keep each other's spirits up so that no one falls behind or drops out."

(Ephesians 6:13-18 THE MESSAGE)

References

1. "Theology of Rape," found at http://ow.ly/WXkLc

2. "Ibadah," http://ow.ly/WXl8M

3. "Sabaya," http://ow.ly/WXlMr , http://ow.ly/WXm0D

4. "Department of Veterans Affairs Report," http://ow.ly/WXlxq

5. "Symptoms of PTSD," http://ow.ly/WXm94

6. "How to Control Emotions," video found at http://ow.ly/WXnxb

7. "The Seven Aspects of Forgiveness," video found at http://ow.ly/WYANs

8. "The Joy of Living by Commandment," video found at http://ow.ly/WXnNw

9. "How to Control Imaginations," video found at http://ow.ly/WXo0B

10. Further information about baptism can be found in Romans 6:4–11 or at http://ow.ly/WXmNG

11. "How to Know You Are a Genuine Christian," video found at http://ow.ly/WXoeb

12. God's Plan for Man, used by permission from Dake Publishing, Inc., page 13, found at http://ow.ly/WYeRz

13. "How to Deal with Fools," video found at http://ow.ly/WXoqB